Pebble® Plus

AMAZING SIGHTS OF THE SKY

Rainbows

by Martha E. H. Rustad

CAPSTONE PRESS
a capstone imprint

Pebble Plus is published by Capstone Press,
1710 Roe Crest Drive, North Mankato, Minnesota 56003
www.mycapstone.com

Library of Congress Cataloging-in-Publication Data
Library of Congress Cataloging-in-Publication data is available on the Library of Congress website.
ISBN: 978-1-5157-6750-3 (library hardcover)
ISBN: 978-1-5157-6756-5 (paperback)
ISBN: 978-1-5157-6768-8 (eBook PDF)

Summary: Simple text introduces readers to the science behind rainbows, including why rainbows occur.

Editorial Credits
Anna Butzer, editor; Juliette Peters, designer; Wanda Winch, media researcher; Steve Walker, production specialist

Photo Credits
iStockphoto: gui00878, 7; Shutterstock: Aluca69, 1, Andrea Izzotti, cover, BILD LLC, 13, Dark Moon Pictures, 17, Felix Nendzig, 19, Lopatko Kyrylo, 21, Massimo Vernicesole, 9, Podfoto, 5, PongMoji, rainbow background, Vitalii Bashkatov, 15; Thinkstock: iStockphoto/ktsimage, 11

Note to Parents and Teachers

The Amazing Sights of the Sky set supports national science standards related to earth science. This book describes and illustrates rainbows. The images support early readers in understanding the text. The repetition of words and phrases helps early readers learn new words. This book also introduces early readers to subject-specific vocabulary words, which are defined in the Glossary section. Early readers may need assistance to read some words and to use the Table of Contents, Glossary, Read More, Internet Sites, Critical Thinking Questions, and Index sections of the book.

Table of Contents

What Are Rainbows?

The raindrops stop falling.

The sun peeks out from

behind the clouds.

Do you see the rainbow?

A rainbow is a curve of colored stripes.

At the top we see red, orange,

yellow, green, and blue.

Then we see indigo and violet.

These colors are shades of purple.

Why Do Rainbows Shine?

Rainbows happen when light shines

through tiny water drops.

Light looks white.

But it is made up of many colors.

The water drops act like a prism.

A prism bends light

and separates the colors.

We see a rainbow.

Sundogs

Sometimes in cold air, we see sundogs.

Light bends through ice crystals

instead of water drops.

This creates two spots of light

to the left and right of the sun.

See a Rainbow

Rainbows appear in the sky

opposite of the sun.

They are easier to see

when the sun is low in the sky.

Rainbows seem to touch
the ground. But they do not.
Our eyes are playing a trick
on our brains.

A double rainbow has
two bands of colors.
The color pattern is backward
in the top rainbow.
Violet is the top color.

To see a rainbow,

wait for a rainy day.

Watch for the rain to stop

and the sun to shine.

You will see an amazing sight!

GLOSSARY

forecast—a prediction for what the weather will be

indigo—a bluish purple color

prism—a piece of glass or plastic; light waves bend when they pass through a prism

sundog—a bright spot that appears on either side of the sun; a sundog is caused by light bending through ice crystals

violet—another word for purple

READ MORE

Beaton, Kathryn. *I See Rainbows.* Tell Me Why. Ann Arbor, Mich.: Cherry Lake Publishing, 2015.

Furstinger, Nancy. *Discovering Prisms.* 3D Objects. New York: AV2 by Weigl, 2017.

Steinberg, Lynnae. *Rainbows and Other Marvels of Light and Water.* Nature's Mysteries. New York: Rosen, 2017.

INTERNET SITES

Use FactHound to find Internet sites related to this book.

Visit *www.facthound.com*

Just type in 9781515767503 and go.

Super-cool stuff! Check out projects, games and lots more at **www.capstonekids.com**

CRITICAL THINKING QUESTIONS

1. What do water drops do to light to make a rainbow?

2. What bends light to make sun dogs?

3. What color is at the top of a rainbow?

INDEX